Ancient Magick for
Today's Witch Series

MOON MAGICK

MONIQUE JOINER SIEDLAK

OSHUN
PUBLICATIONS
oshunpublications.com

Moon Magick © 2015 by Monique Joiner Siedlak

ISBN 978-1-948834-52-0 (Paperback)

ISBN 978-1-948834-53-7 (eBook)

Cover Design by MJS

Cover Images by MidJourney

Published by Oshun Publications

www.oshunpublications.com

Ancient Magick for Today's Witch Series

The *Ancient Magick for Today's Witch Series* is a series for modern witches to explore ancient magick, covering Celtic, Gypsy, and Crystal magic, among others. It offers practical advice on spells, rituals, and enchantments for today's use, incorporating natural energies and spiritual connections. With insights into Shamanism, Wicca, and more, it helps readers enhance their magickal journey, offering paths to protection, prosperity, and spiritual growth by combining ancient wisdom with contemporary practice.

Wiccan Basics
Candle Magick
Wiccan Spells
Love Spells
Abundance Spells
Herb Magick
Moon Magick
Creating Your Own Spells
Gypsy Magic
Protection Magick
Celtic Magick

Shamanic Magick
Crystal Magic
Sacred Spaces
Solitary Witchcraft
Novice Witch's Guide

AVAILABLE IN AUDIO!

GYPSY MAGIC

MONIQUE JOINER SIEDLAK

mojosiedlak.com/audiobooks

MONIQUE JOINER SIEDLAK
GET UPDATES,
FREEBIES &
GIVEAWAYS
JOIN MY NEWSLETTER
MOJOSIEDLAK.COM/MOONLIGHT-MUSINGS

Contents

Introduction

The moon is a celestial body man has used as a tool since the times of cave dwellers. Stone carvings and cave art have been found that show early humans used the moon to track time. Man has been obsessed with the moon from ancient times. Poems, nursery rhymes, and songs are written about it, and it plays a part in almost every horror movie written. Man has even raced to be the first to land on the moon. And let's not forget that when you were a kid, you probably thought the man on the moon was watching you. The moon was made from Swiss cheese because of the dark craters in it (Our Ancient Obsession with Capturing the Moon, 2019).

Scientifically speaking, the moon has an immense influence over the Earth and affects the ocean's tides because of its gravitational pull on the planet. The moon takes around 29.5 days to completely orbit the Earth, doing so in a counterclockwise rotation. The moon rotates around the Earth at an average speed of up to 2,300 miles per hour. The moon travels the same time to spin about its own axis as it progresses around the Earth. Because of the time it takes to orbit its own axis, only one side of the moon ever faces the Earth. The moon's hemisphere, which faces away from the Earth, is known as the dark side of the moon (Facts About the Moon, 2004).

The moon's dark or far side is called the lunar side of the moon, which is not actually that dark at all. A lunar day lasts for up to one month, baking the moon's lunar side at temperatures of up to 243° Fahrenheit for periods of two weeks at a time. Therefore, the moon's dark side is airless and dry; there are no indigenous water sources on the moon. As hot as the dark side can get for two weeks, it can get even colder for another two when it descends into darkness. When the moon's lunar side moves into two weeks of darkness, it cools down to temperatures of up to -272° Fahrenheit (Facts About the Moon, 2004).

If one gazes up at the moon from the Earth, what can be regarded as the man in the moon is really giant pits in the moon. Scars left from objects that hit into its surface, leaving craters and rocky rubble centuries ago.

During each month of the year, the moon changes shape in what appears to be a cyclic rotation called lunar phases or the moon's phases. The different aspects of the moon hold a considerable influence over the Earth like the tides, as discussed above. It is not only the planet that is affected by the different phases of the moon. It is also the creatures on it. Animals, including human beings, are deeply affected. Hence the sayings about moon madness and why people sometimes do crazy things during a full moon. The moon has an effect on human emotions during certain phases of it. It influences astrology and affects how a witch's magick spells will work; some spells work better during specific cycles of the moon.

This book explores the various phases of the moon and introduces you to its magic. By the end of the book, you will have a better understanding of the moon's phases, eclipses, and how they work together to create powerful moon magic.

ONE

Moon Phases

THE MOON'S SHAPE SEEMS TO CHANGE WHEN VIEWED FROM THE Earth because you can only see portions of the moon. This is because of the moon's positioning between the Earth and the sun at various times of the month. If you thought of the sun like a giant spotlight being shone on the moon, then when the sun is immediately behind the Earth (the Earth is directly between the sun and the moon), it ultimately illuminates the moon, showing a full moon.

There are four main phases of the moon, which are called lunar phases. The moon shapes appear to vary in size at different times of the month from Earth because of where the moon is positioned to both the sun and the Earth. The new moon is the direct opposite of the full moon as the sun's spotlight is shining from behind the moon. The moon, immediately between the sun and the Earth through the new moon phase, is barely visible, if at all, to the Earth.

As the moon passes through the four phases, it will slowly become more visible (waxing) until it is full. From the full moon, its visibility will start to fade away in quarters (waning) until it becomes a new moon.

New Moon

The new moon is when the moon lines directly between the Earth and the sun. This means the sun is behind the moon, illuminating its dark side so it cannot be seen from Earth. The new moon is considered as being the start of the moon's cycle as it once again starts its journey around the Earth.

Waxing Moon

When the moon passes into the waxing period, it slowly becomes more visible in the night sky in different crescent shapes. As the moon moves into a better position around the Earth, it becomes more visible and can be seen in the sky when the sun goes down right up until sunrise the following day.

There are a few different waxing moon phases associated with this phase:

- Waxing Crescent — This will appear a few days after the new moon as it travels east and becomes better illuminated. It shows as a slight crescent or edge of the crescent; it looks like a sliver of the moon.
- First Quarter — This will appear as a half-moon and is called the first quarter because the moon has finished the first quarter of its lunar cycle.
- Waxing Gibbous — This is the phase where the moon looks like it is almost full and can sometimes appear like the last edge of it has been clipped off. It is the phase directly before the full moon.

Full Moon

The full moon is the big, bright moon that can sometimes seem so enormous that it is expanded out in front of you, touching down to the Earth below. It is when the moon is the most visible from the Earth, which lies directly between it and the sun. On days of the full moon, you notice that the moon may remain in the sky during the morning. In the western sky, it will set as soon as the sun rises and rise as quickly as the sunsets.

Waning Moon

After the full moon lunar phase, it will start to wane as it continues onto the third quarter of its journey around the Earth. The moon will no longer be in the best position to be illuminated, so it looks like minor pieces of it start to fade away.

There are a few different waning moon phases associated with this phase:

- Waning Gibbous — This is the phase where the moon looks like it is almost full, but a portion of it has been cut away. It is much like the Waxing Gibbous, but the side that will fade is the opposite side to the Waxing Gibbous.
- Third Quarter — This will appear as a half-moon and is called the third quarter because the moon has finished the third quarter of its lunar cycle. The visible half will be the exact opposite of the half that became visible during the First Quarter moon.
- Waning Crescent — This will appear as a sliver or small crescent of the moon before it descends into the new moon's darkness. Once again, the crescent will appear on the opposite side of what emerged during the Waxing Crescent moon.

Blue Moon

A blue moon is a phenomenon that rarely happens, hence the term "once in a blue moon."

There are also three different definitions of a blue moon:

Seasonal Blue Moon

This was the first astronomical definition of a blue moon

where there are four full moons between each astronomical season. An astronomical season is a time between a solstice and an equinox; usually, there are only three full moons within this period. Whenever there are four full moons in the period, the fourth one is called the blue moon.

Monthly Blue Moon

There is usually one full moon during a monthly cycle (a lunar month; that is, the time between two full moons). Every once in a while, a lunar month will have two full moons. The second full moon of that month will be called a blue moon.

The full moon is often named after the season or some seasonal event in some northern hemisphere cultures, like the harvest moon. Thus, a second full moon in the same month is called a blue moon and only happens every two to three years.

The Rare Blue Moon

One of the rarest of all moons is a full moon that looks blue. This usually only happens on a full moon when there have been volcanic eruptions, a tremendous forest fire, or a dust storm. These phenomena leave particles that are larger than 900 nm in the atmosphere called Mie scatterings, which makes the moon look blue.

Blood Moon

A blood moon occurs during a complete lunar eclipse of the full moon. The reflective rays of the sunlight cause the moon to appear red. How red the moon appears depends on the amount of dust, even pollution in the air, and particles in the atmosphere.

Supermoon

A supermoon is when the moon looks that much more prominent and brighter in the sky. This occurs when a full moon happens while the moon's orbital path brings it closer to Earth. Because the moon's orbit is not always smooth, super-moons do not occur that often; they may only happen a few times a year.

TWO

Full Moon Names and Correspondences

THE FULL MOON HAS BEEN GIVEN DISTINCTIVE NAMES throughout the year by numerous cultures. To name a few of these cultures are Old English, Celtic, and New Guinea and Chinese. The Full Moon names were applied to classify the entire month during which each occurred with the Native American tribes.

The following names given are not the only names that have been used. With only one exclusion, every Full Moon has had adaptations on its name between tribes all through North America. Nevertheless, the following names are the most common as well as some of the alternatives.

January

Gender: Feminine

Other Names: Birch Moon, Cold Moon, Frost Moon, Old Moon, Wolf Moon

This is the moon to develop your inner self and purify water for Imbolc. It is the time to review your goals. Since this is a protective month, create your protective sachets. Schedule a ritual of protection for your family and home.

Colors: Black, White, Silver
Herbs and plants: Basil, Marjoram, Nuts, Seeds
Stones: Hematite, Quartz, Snowflake Obsidian
Element: Air

February

Gender: Masculine

Other Names: Hunger Moon, Ice Moon, Rowan Moon, Quickening Moon, Snow Moon, Storm Moon, Wild Moon

This is the perfect moon for renewals. It is time to finish any tasks that are currently ongoing in order to make way for the new beginnings in your life. Focus on the goals that involve personal development. Above all, take responsibility for any mistakes. Engage in some meditation and astral travel. Plan a ritual to ask the Old Ones for help in developing your future.

Colors: Purple, Blue
Herbs and Plants: Hyssop, Myrrh, Sage
Stones: Amethyst, Jasper, Rose Quartz
Element: Fire

March

Gender: Feminine

Other Names: Ash Moon, Chaste Moon, Hare Moon, Storm Moon, Worm Moon

This is the moon to look at your financial goals and create balance in your life. Perform luck and money spells. Plan a ritual to help fulfill your wishes is suitable.

Colors: Green, Lavender, Yellow
Herbs and Plants: Betony, High John the Conqueror, Thyme
Stones: Aquamarine, Bloodstone
Element: Water

April

Gender: Masculine
Other Names: Alder Moon, Growing Moon, Pink Moon, Seed Moon
Think about your knowledge goals during this moon. Right now is the time to create vast changes in your existence. It is also a wonderful period to perform Candle Magick
Colors: Blue, Red, Yellow
Herbs and Plants: Dandelion, Dill, Dogwood, Fennel
Stones: Angelite, Quartz, Selenite
Element: Air

May

Gender: Feminine
Other Names: Flower Moon, Hare Moon, Merry Moon, Willow Moon
This is the moon to focus on your career goals. Look for growth from within during this time. Plan a ritual to confirm your goals and perform job spells.
Colors: Orange, Red, Yellow
Herbs and Plants: Cinnamon, Mint
Stones: Amber, Apache Tear, Garnet
Element: Fire

June

Gender: Masculine
Other Names: Hawthorn Moon, Honey Moon, Mead Moon, Strawberry Moon
Think about your goals during this is the moon involving organization and cleaning. Prepare a six-month review of your yearly goals. Perform cleansing spells and rituals to balance your spiritual and physical desires.

Colors: Gold, Orange, Yellow
Herbs and Plants: Moss, Mugwort, Parsley
Stones: Agate, Topaz
Element: Earth

July

Gender: Masculine
Other Names: Blessing Moon, Buck Moon, Mead Moon, Oak Moon, Wort Moon
This is the moon Plan a ritual to decide what you will do once your goals have been met.
Look at your goals about vacation or hobbies. Find a period to meditate and relax.
Colors: Blue, Blue-Gray, Gray, Green, Silver
Herbs and Plants: Chamomile, Hyssop, Lemon
Stones: Moonstone, Opal, White Agate
Element: Water

August

Gender: Feminine
Other Names: Corn Moon, Holly Moon, Sturgeon Moon, Wyrt Moon
This is the moon you should focus on your goals involving health and wellness. The sacrifices you make now will be beneficial later. Plan a ritual to keep what you already have.
Colors: Orange, Red, Yellow
Herbs and Plants: Basil, Catnip, Rosemary
Stones: Carnelian, Red Agate, Tiger's Eye
Element: Fire

September

Gender: Feminine
Other Names: Barley Moon, Harvest Moon, Hazel Moon
This moon that encourages us all to examine the balance in our lives and deal with any changes still needs to take place. Look to the goals surrounding your home and those within it. Prepare for the winter. Time to set up your kitchen altar and engage in food and herbal magick.
Colors: Brown, Green
Herbs and Plants: Flax Seed, Wheat, Witch Hazel
Stones: Bloodstone, Citrine, Peridot
Element: Earth

October

Gender: Feminine and Masculine
Other Names: Blood Moon, Hunter's Moon, Vine Moon
Plan a ritual in the course of this moon to remember those who have passed from this world. Look to and learn from ancestors and those passed. Remember to make an offering to them. Ponder on your goals that involve spiritual advancement. Consider working on scrying and dream work.
Colors: Black, Dark Blue, Purple
Herbs and Plants: Apple Blossom, Mint, Rose
Stones: Amethyst, Obsidian, Tourmaline
Element: Air

November

Gender: Masculine
Other Names: Beaver Moon, Dark Moon, Frost Moon, Ivy Moon, Snow Moon
This is the moon Plan for a ritual to work on ridding your-

self of negative thoughts and vibrations with a banishing spell. You may also revisit your goals.

Colors: Blue Gray

Herbs and Plants: Betony, Fennel, Pepper, Thistle

Stones: Lapis Lazuli, Topaz, Turquoise

Element: Water

December

Gender: Masculine

Other Names: Birch Moon, Cold Moon, Elder Moon, Oak Moon

This is the moon to plan for a ritual to help you remain unwavering in your principles. Make new goals for the next twelve months. Share your happiness with others and donate volunteer or do both. Work on your gemstone magick

Colors: Black, Red, White

Herbs and Plants: Cinnamon, Ivy, Mistletoe Berries

Stones: Obsidian, Ruby, Serpentine

Element: Earth

Blue Moon

Gender: Feminine and Masculine

Other Names: Thirteenth Moon

This is the moon of self-improvement. Make your wishes and cast your spells under the Blue Moon, especially if you are focusing on long-term results. Your goals will have until the next Blue Moon to develop. In 2018, there will be a Blue Moon in January, with another one two months later in March. Get ready!

Colors: Black, Purple, White

Herbs and Plants: Ginger, Nutmeg

Stones: Obsidian Onyx, Quartz

Element: Spirit

Updated: The next Blue Moon occurrence will be October 31, 2020. However, on May 18, 2019, there will be a Seasonal Blue Moon. The seasonal blue moon refers to the third full moon in a season giving it four full moons.

THREE

Eclipses

THE MOON'S LUNAR PHASES APPEAR TO CHANGE THE MOON'S shape because moonlight is actually a reflection of the sun shining on the moon's white/gray surface. Now and then, the moon will fall into the Earth's shadow, or the Earth will fall into the moon's shadow, creating an eclipse of the sun.

There are two main types of eclipses:

Lunar Eclipse

The lunar eclipse occurs during the night and usually late in the evening.

A lunar eclipse occurs when the moon falls into the Earth's shadow. This blocks out the moonlight as it passes through the Earth's shadow. Throughout this time, the moon seems to be a blood-red color. This is due to a slight amount of sunlight shining through from around the edges of the Earth.

Lunar eclipses only appear roughly twice a year because of the way the moon orbits the Earth while the Earth orbits the sun. At specific times of the year, the moon is positioned in such a way it passes through the Earth's shadow.

There are two types of lunar eclipses:

- The total eclipse — This is when the moon is completely blocked by the Earth's shadow. During a total eclipse, the Earth is in between the sun and moon.
- The partial eclipse is when only a bit of the Earth's shadow is covering the moon.

Solar Eclipse

A solar eclipse happens during the day.

The new moon lunar phase is the only time a solar eclipse can happen. It is during the new moon that the moon falls between the Earth and the sun. However, because of the moon's tilt on its orbit around the Earth, like a lunar eclipse, the moon has to move in precise alignment for an eclipse to happen. Typically, in relation to the Earth's orbit around the sun, the moon orbits the Earth at a tilt of five degrees. At this tilt, when the new moon rises, the Earth does not fall into the moon's shadow. But at least twice a year as the Earth orbits the sun and the moon orbits the Earth, the Earth falls into the moon's shadow. When this happens, the moon blocks out the sunlight as the Earth passes through the moon's shadow.

Solar eclipses can seem a little complex because while one part of the Earth may see a total eclipse, another part witnessing the same event will only see a partial eclipse. This is because the moon casts two shadows: the umbra and penumbra.

- The umbra is the darkened center of the moon's shadow that becomes smaller as it reflects onto the Earth. The place on Earth that is covered by the umbra will see a total eclipse.
- The penumbra is the shadow that will expand, getting more significant as it reaches the Earth. People who live in areas shadowed by the penumbra will only get to see a partial eclipse.

There are four types of solar eclipses:

- The total eclipse — This is when the moon completely blocks out the sun.
- The partial eclipse is when the umbral shadow does not hit the Earth, and it passes through the moon's penumbral shadow. This usually makes the sun look like a sickle.
- The annular eclipse — The word annulus is from Latin and means ring or ring-like. This kind of eclipse is when the moon's shadow blocks out the center of the sun, leaving only a circle of its rays visible around the moon's shape.
- The hybrid eclipse — The hybrid eclipse is rare and happens when half of the earth witnesses a total eclipse while the other half sees an annular eclipse.

FOUR

Moon Phase Magick

THE NEAREST BODY TO THE EARTH IS THE MOON IN THE VAST expanse of the dark universe that looms above us. It is both a protector and an influencer to the Earth, having a strong influence over everything on the planet. The moon is what lightens dark nights, is the reason the tides ebb and flow, and marks milestones in a month, season, or year. It also prevents catastrophic events like the Earth spinning off as it stabilizes the 23.5-degree tilt of the Earth's axis.

Between the sun and the moon, the Earth is nourished and nurtured as these two great bodies lend their power to all life on Earth. The waxing moon phase is one of the first phases after the new moon. It is the time the moon moved from the new moon where it is barely, if at all, visible to the first crescent then onto to the first quarter, after which it flows to the waxing gibbous.

This part of the lunar phase is the time of growth. It is when what was started in the new moon phase starts to take root and grow. If you look at moon magick as planting a tree, the new moon would be planting the seed, and the waxing moon would see that seed starting to get roots and then sprout. Your intentions are taking hold of what you sought at the new moon and creating a solid foundation for it to grow as it stretches out towards the full moon.

Each new moon, you get to refreshes your cycle and cleanses your soul. But the moon cannot do all the work for you; it takes effort, commitment, and follow-through for you. Your intentions have just started to grow within the universe; you need to push through and keep going. If things are looking rough, you can't give up; you have to keep nurturing your intentions, or they will not grow.

Moon magick is about giving thanks to the moon for its light, protection, and draws on the power each phase of the moon offers.

New Moon Magick: Beginning

The new moon is the beginning of a new lunar cycle and brings the opportunity to start fresh, wash away negative energies, and begin again. It is a time for new wishes, letting go of baggage that is dragging you down, and initiation.

At the start of the new moon, you will be bathed in the light of the moon's intentions as it offers its strength, courage, and power. You can harness these energies to purge negative thoughts, habits, and anything holding you back from achieving your goals. As the moon grows through its lunar phases, moving from strength to strength, your intentions will grow with it until the next new moon.

The new moon is an exceptional time to:

- Start new projects
- Start new lifestyles
- Start a new career
- Let go of things pulling you down
- Release things that no longer serve you
- Make a wish
- Move to a new home
- Any new beginning

The new moon is time to take stock of:

- Your desires
- Your hopes
- Your dreams
- Your fears
- Your current situation

The new moon is the time you need to commit to:

- Letting go of fear
- Having faith in yourself
- Finding your inner voice
- Listening to your inner voice
- Trusting your inner voice
- Visualizing your intentions

The following gemstones can help you harness the energies of the new moon:

- Clear Quartz
- Black Moonstone
- Labradorite
- Obsidian

Waxing Moon Magick: Growth

The waxing moon phase is one of the first phases after the new moon. It is the time the moon moved from the new moon where it is barely, if at all, visible to the first crescent then onto to the first quarter, after which it flows to the Waxing Gibbous.

This part of the lunar phase is the time of growth. It is the time when what was started in the new moon phase starts to take root and grow. The seed of intention you planted at the new moon has taken root and started to grow. Your plans are taking hold of what you sought at the new moon and creating a solid foundation for it to grow as it stretches out towards the full moon.

During each waxing moon, you need to ensure you follow through with your intentions as the moon cannot do all the work for you. You need to practice patience, perseverance, and self-discipline. If things are looking rough, you can't give up; you have to keep nurturing your intentions to make sure they grow to fruition.

The waxing moon is an excellent opportunity to:

- Let go of the old
- Keep pushing forward
- Renew your commitment to your goals
- Stay strong
- Be courageous
- Be open to the universe
- Accept positive energy
- Don't give up
- Try and try again if need be
- Get creative
- Make the most of your imagination

The waxing moon is time to take stock of:

- Your commitment and heart's content
- Start throwing away clutter
- What works best for you to help you keep moving forward
- Who you really are

The waxing moon is the time you need to commit to:

- Your intentions
- Your desires
- Your goals

- Strengthening your resolve
- Your mindfulness
- Courage
- Perseverance
- Embracing your true inner self

The following gemstones can help you harness the energies of the waxing moon:

- Citrine
- Diopside
- Emerald
- Fluorite
- Jet
- Nuummite
- Onyx

Full Moon Magick: Your Heart's Desire

At the new moon, a person sets forth their intentions and releases their desire to the universe by drawing the moon's help. As she phases through the waxing stage, she guides and helps you grow those intentions and desires while lending her power. At the full moon stage, we see the new moon in her full glory shining down proudly for all to marvel at. This is when she is at her full strength, a strength that flows through to you, giving you the power to reveal your heart's desires. You are ready to reap the rewards of your hard work, perseverance, and persistence.

Although the full moon is a time to rejoice, it is also a time to take care as you may be able to control and harness the full force of your magick, but others may not be able to control theirs. Those who hold onto bad energy may be affected negatively; it is best to avoid such people at this time.

The full moon is an excellent chance to:

- Rejoice in the universe
- Rejoice in yourself
- Reap the rewards of your hard work
- Give yourself a break
- Enjoy what you have brought forth

The full moon is time to take stock of:

- Your life at this point
- How you are going to move forward
- How to keep the negative forces at bay
- The next challenges ahead

The full moon is the time you need to commit to:

- Rejoicing in your achievements
- Letting go of failures but not of the lessons learned from them
- Keeping those with a negative influence at arm's length
- Moving forward, harnessing only positive energies
- Making sure you are always moving forward
- Never looking back

The following gemstones can help you harness the energies of the full moon:

- Moonstone
- Quartz
- Selenite

Waning Moon Magick: Purging

As the moon starts her slide into the final stages of its lunar phase for the current cycle, it is time to reflect on your current status. It is time to figure out what more can be purged and what can be given back to the universe in thanks for what you have been fortunate enough to receive. It is time to pay it forward, so to speak by letting go of that which does not serve you and giving back to those in need.

You need to purge what greed or impurities you hold onto so you can move into the next cycle of rebirth. It is a period of self-reflection and sacrifice for the welfare of the new generation and your renewal through the next new moon. You crave to give the best of yourself to those around you while you get rid of the worst of yourself.

The waxing moon is an excellent period to:

- Show love
- Show compassion
- Give with your whole heart
- Reflect on who you are
- Know who you want to be

The waxing moon is time to take stock of:

- Who you are
- What no longer serves your happiness
- Your relationships
- Negative influences

The waxing moon is the time you need to commit to:

- Sacrificing the best part of you
- Purging negative energies and influences
- Working on the worst part of yourself
- Getting in touch with your soul
- Giving love and being open to receiving it
- Keeping an open heart and mind

The following gemstones can help you harness the energies of the waxing moon:

- Bronzite
- Calcite
- Obsidian
- Rose Quartz

Dark Moon Magick: A Respite

There is quite a bit of uncertainty between the new moon and the dark moon. Some new-age practitioners of various forms of magick refer to what should be the dark as the new moon.

During ancient times when people looked to the skies for their answers, the dark moon was the period of rest between the waning moon and the new moon. It is the period of a few days when the moon is not visible; it is said to be at rest after its journey around the Earth. While the new moon starts when you can see the first sliver of the moon, it starts to move into the waxing phase. This phase was known as the horns of Isis to the ancient Egyptians.

The dark moon is a time for respite, a time to relax, regain your strength, and breathe as you complete this cycle. Go for long walks, take note of the world around you. Slow down, and remember to look up at the heavens and smell the roses along the way.

The dark moon is an excellent time to/for:

- Meditate
- Soul searching
- Cleansing
- Purifying
- Smudging
- Detoxification
- Rest

- Contemplation
- Release
- Inner silence and peace

The dark moon is time to take stock of:

- Your spells
- Your rituals
- Your magick tools
- Your inner circle
- Your peace of mind

The dark moon is the time you need to commit to:

- Setting new goals
- Personal growth
- New blessings
- Renewal
- Rejuvenation
- Fresh starts
- Having a clear focus

The following gemstones can help you harness the energies of the dark moon:

- Fluorite
- Kyanite
- Peach Moonstone
- Red Tigers Eye

FIVE

Magick During Eclipses

ECLIPSES HAVE A POTENT EFFECT ON MAGICK. THE MOON AND the sun are powerful enhancements that are drawn on to enhance a person's magic. During an eclipse, all three astrological bodies are in perfect alignment, which magnifies their energy to the earth. This affects all living things on earth in one way or the other. Most people do not feel it or instead don't acknowledge it while those more sensitive to its powers do.

Some practitioners of magick will not practice their craft when these celestial events occur. They feel that if the forces are not properly harnessed, it can cause their magick to go awry. But for those that can harness the eclipse's power, be it a solar or lunar one, will feel their magick be intensified.

Solar Eclipses

A solar eclipse is about new beginnings and endings. It is a time of change that will happen quickly and, therefore, it is a time to initiate a change that needs a quick turnaround, for instance, finding relief for stress, needing help making a tough decision, and so on.

For magick to work during a solar eclipse, you will need to know the exact time of the eclipse and make sure you are prepared ahead of time. You do not have long to prepare the ritual, nor do you have long to perform. The ritual needs to be kept short, mindful, and to the point.

Keep the area around you well smudged and free from the chaos of powerful energies colliding. Do not perform magick for others during a solar eclipse as the sun and moon magnify these energies. If it goes awry, there could be severe consequences for the practitioner.

During the lunar eclipse, it is time to reflect on:

- What needs an immediate change in your life or circumstances
- What your immediate needs or desires are
- What you need to get rid of with immediate effect
- If you are on the correct paths or do, you need to change lanes quickly

The lunar eclipse is time to take stock of:

- Your life
- Your job
- Your surroundings
- Any negative energies
- Any negative influences
- Self-doubt
- Your dreams
- If you are where you want to be at this moment

The lunar eclipse is the time you need to commit to:

- Making immediate changes to your circumstances or life
- Letting go of anyone or anything that has a negative influence on you

- Letting go of immediate subconscious or conscious blockages
- Purging anything that is bringing you down
- Purging anything that is making you stressed, anxious, or unhappy
- Working on improving yourself, your lifestyle, and your surroundings

The following gemstones can help you harness the energies of the dark moon:

- Dark Moonstone
- Labradorite
- Moonstone
- Sunstone

Lunar Eclipses

A lunar eclipse is associated with a change to a person's mental and physical being. It emphasizes one's emotions as well as physical health. That is why magick practitioners refer to the lunar eclipse as being identified with the emotional and physical body. Any rituals or intentions being set forth need to relate to the practitioner's physical self and not that of another person. All practitioners of magick live by the code of doing no harm, do what ye will. But if harm to another is done, it will come back to the practitioner tenfold.

Like with a solar eclipse, a lunar eclipse will intensify a person's magick by making it twice as strong as well as happening twice as fast. If you practice magick for someone else during this period and the magick goes awry, you will suffer the consequences twice tenfold over.

This is the same for a solar eclipse and is why a practitioner will only work magick for themselves during an eclipse. It is crucial to be conscious of this. Many practitioners will not go anywhere near magick during a lunar eclipse, believing that when the world descends to darkness, their powers need to be put to rest. Some even believe they have no power during this time, and to try force their power is tapping into the dark arts.

Before you begin the ritual to practice magick before a lunar eclipse, make sure you know the exact time of the event. Smudge the areas you are working in correctly and draw the protective circle at least five minutes before the time. Make sure you are well prepared with your alter at the ready. Start the ritual early enough to have to harness the full power of the eclipse.

Call upon those that protect you, and keep them in your light as the moon descends into darkness. Always keep sight of the fact that an eclipse happens during a full moon, which in itself is a very powerful source of magick. It is also magick that will have quick results.

During the lunar eclipse, it is time to reflect on:

- Self-image
- Self-awareness
- Your emotional state
- How others perceive you
- How you want others to perceive you
- Your mental health
- Your emotions health
- Your physical health

The lunar eclipse is time to take stock of:

- Your health and any issues you may be having
- Your weight
- Your physical fitness
- Your lifestyle choices
- Your relationship
- Your family

The lunar eclipse is the time you need to commit to:

- Your physical well-being
- Your emotional well-being
- Making positive lifestyle changes
- Making better personal choices
- Connecting with your loved ones
- Building bridges

The following gemstones can help you harness the energies of the dark moon:

- Amethyst
- Black Moonstone
- Peach Moonstone
- Rainbow Moonstone
- Rose Quartz
- Tourmaline
- White Moonstone

SIX

New Moon Spells

Love Spell Box

ITEMS NEEDED

    A Box
    Red candle
    Black candle
    Love Objects
    Glue

Directions

On a New Moon start a search to find "love" objects to place inside the box, collecting nine objects. Charge them with your personal love energy. Place the objects and your box on your altar. Light the red and black candles. Pick up each object in your dominant hand and visualize the strongest emotions you have ever felt while in love. Glue each item into the box so that it stays in place. Let your intuition guide you to where to place each object. If you have a specific person in mind place, his/her picture in the box as well. Conceal the box in a magickal location in your home. Every once in a while open the box to reenergize the items while allowing some of the energy inside move out into you.

New Moon Job Spell

Items needed
2 Green Candles
2 Gold Candles
2 Pieces Tiger Eye
2 Pieces of Malachite
2 White Candles
Cinnamon Oil

Directions
Alternating the colors, arrange the candles in a line, anoint each candle with cinnamon oil, and dab a little oil on your stones. Begin at one end and light each candle. As you light each one, say:

"It is a new career I desire,
I cast this spell to secure a hire.
By the darkness of this New Moon,
I want a new job soon."

Once all the candles are lit, take each stone with your dominant hand and gently pass it through the flames. At that time hold the stones in your hands and create in your mind the kind of job you want to get. Afterward, take the stones and carry them with you. You should have a new position by the following New Moon.

New Moon Money Charm

Items needed

2 Green Candles
1 Orange Candle
Green Drawstring Bag
Lodestone or Magnet
Picture of Yourself

Nutmeg

Marjoram

Thyme

Fake Paper Money

Dragons Blood Incense (or any type of money drawing incense)

Directions

To be performed Thursday in the hour of Jupiter

Place your items on your altar. Cleanse and consecrate your sacred area and items you will be using. Ignite the incense as you focus and concentrate. Say:

"New Moon, New Moon,

When the moon is new

Bless me with prosperities hearth!

On this night of your re-birth,

I plant the seeds, I let them sow,

Into fruition, my fortune grows.

Grant me a wide fortunes field,

With your power, riches yield."

Take a bit of the candle wax from both candle and drip onto your photo. Set the lodestone or magnet into the wax. Place into the bag. Grasp the fake paper money into your hands and recite three times:

"This paper money comes alive

And my fortune start to rise"

Put the fake paper money into the drawstring bag, and pull the strings of the bag shut. Pass the drawstring bag in the smoke from the incense and say:

"By harming none, on its way,

Make my fortune here to stay.

Through the sky, heavens, and earth,

Return my money, on this eve's rebirth."

Your charm is completed. Take the bag with you always.

New Moon Manifestation

Items needed
Candle
Pen
Paper

Directions
Write down what you would like to manifest for example your hopes, dreams, and wants. Write them with a strong impression of **I WILL, I AM**, etc.

Read your list aloud to the New Moon. Once you have completed, give thanks to the universe, gods and or goddesses for listening. Fold your list toward you and keep it in a safe place.

Every day, read your list outside thanking the moon and the universe, gods and or goddesses until the moon is full.

Once the moon is full, take your candle with you and read your list on last time. Light your candle and burn your list. Trust that it will be provided.

New Moon Wishing Spell

Items needed
Candle
Paper
Pen

Directions
In the evening of the New Moon, take your items outside locating a quiet area that you will not be interrupted. Light your candle. Gazing into the flame, reflect on your wish. Write your wish on your paper. Closing your eyes, visualize your wish coming true. Believe, see and know that it will come true. Feel it will come true. Gaze up into the night sky letting the New Moon's power to cloak you. Ask the universe, gods and

or goddesses to grant your wish is it is for the Higher Good of all. Remember to thank Her/Him/Them.

Burn the paper in the candle. Your spell is complete.

New Moon Ritual Bath

Items needed

10 drops Lemon Essential Oil

$\frac{1}{2}$ cup Himalayan Sea Salt

$\frac{1}{2}$ cup Sage Leaves

White Candle

Pen

Paper

Directions

On a piece of paper, write down your New Moon goals. Begin the water for your bath and light your white candle. Add the remainder of items to the bath. Go into your bath and visualize your energy being revitalized.

SEVEN

Waxing Moon Spells

Spell To Attract a Lover with No One Particular in Mind

ITEMS NEEDED

1 tsp. Catnip
1 tsp. Coriander
1 tsp. Ginger
1 tsp. Rosemary
1 tsp. Yarrow

Directions

Blend herbs together. On a Friday at sunset when the moon is waxing, toss into a burning fire. As the herbs burn, say:

"The face of my true love, I have yet to see.

I don't know what his (or her) name could be.

But before long his (her) heart will beat for me.

Come to me, my love.

As my will, so may it be."

Spell to Increase Cash Flow

Item needed:

One Aventurine Gemstone

Directions

To raise your business cash flow, grasp the piece of Aventurine in your dominant hand during the waxing Moon. Focus on money pouring into your business, and cast an attraction within the stone by stating:

"As Money come, money grows;

Increase my money flow.

Fill my cash drawer to the top

Afterward may it by no means stop."

Set the stone in your cash drawer, register or bank bag.

EIGHT

Full Moon Spells

Luck Spell

DIRECTIONS

When the moon is full, speak these words:
"Lady of Luck come out of your veiled path
Send your light on to me
As the beam of the moon shines above
And in the light of luck, I will be blessed,
After the moon is full again."

Full Moon Goal Spell

Items needed

Flowering Plant that has not blossomed or Flower Seeds
Pot
Potting mix
Green candle
Pen
Paper

Directions

On the night of the Full Moon, find an area where you

will not be disturbed. Light your green candle. Write your goal down on the paper. Fill the pot with potting mix, leaving space for plant or holes for seeds. Say:

"Green candle bring fruitful growth

The goal I set here does bring forth."

Pass your plant or seeds through the flame three times with your dominant hand. Say

"Awaken now dormant flowers

With you bring my goal with Nature's power."

Place the paper in the soil and plant your plant or seeds. Say:

"This goal will take root and steadily grow

With each new bud, its movement grows

In full flower I tend

As my goals prosperous end."

The same as you would tend and look after your goals, look after your plant every single day. Talk with your plant about its growth and your goals, tend and care, caress and love it.

Full Moon Money Spell

Items needed

Green Candle

Sandalwood or Patchouli Essential Oil (optional)

Pin or Small Knife

Directions

On the green candle, inscribe the names of the individuals that will be taking part. If you want, anoint the candle with either the Sandalwood or Patchouli essential oil. As you do this, say:

"Now is the time for weaving our wills.

As the Gods and Goddesses

Give us their power,

We pull it into for our use.

We toss our energies into the universe
To build our destinies
As we would have them be."
Light your candle. Concentrate on the energies being sent into it and changed. As they seep past the smoke and flames into power to do your request, say:
"Full Moon that is bright, Full Moon by your light,
Give to me, my wish tonight.
Bring wealth into my life to stay,
Let all my problems melt away.
Allow money come forward now to me.
With harm to none, so mote it be."
Allow your candle to burn out by itself.

Full Moon Love Spell

Items needed
Pink Candle
Red Candle
Dried Basil
Ground Cinnamon
Two Apple Seeds
Rose Quartz Crystal
Moonstone Gemstone
Pink Yarn or Cord
Red Cloth
Directions
Beneath the Full Moon, Collect all the items you need in your sacred space, and cast your circle. Light both your candles and lay the red cloth in front of you. With your dominant hand, take the moonstone, pass it over the flames of both candles, and afterward place the gemstone on the cloth. Repeat this for the rose quartz. At this point, take the two apple seeds, and say:
"Using the light of the Full Moon,

I hereby plant the seeds of our love."

Visualize As you set the seeds on the cloth, beside the crystals, soft pink energy coming from the crystals, feeding the seeds with its loving energy. Dust the stones and seeds with the cinnamon and basil. Finally, draw the corners of the red cloth together, with the seeds, stones, and herbs inside. Wrap the pink cord or yarn about the bag three times, in advance of tying it with three knots.

Say:

"So mote it be."

Close your circle. Keep your charm bag near you at all times in order to draw love into your life.

Full Moon Money Bath

Items needed

3 Parts Dried Basil

1 Part Cinnamon

1 Part Clove

Cloth Sachet Bag

Directions

Begin a warm bath then place all the ingredients in the sachet bag. Make your bath as warm as you can tolerate. Immerse the sachet in the water, allowing it to steep. During the Full Moon bathe in this concoction to increase your vibrations on the spiritual plane so that money will be drawn to you.

As you soak, imagine your bank account, wallet, and bills being met. Drain the bath once the water turns cold, and then bury the contents of your sachet straightaway.

Full Moon Oil

Items needed

13 drops Sandalwood Essential Oil

9 drops Vanilla Essential Oil

3 drops Jasmine Essential Oil

1 drop Rose Essential Oil

One Clear Vial

Directions

This should be mixed in advance of a Full Moon. Once blended, charge your oil in a clear vial in the light of the Full Moon.

This oil can be used to anoint your candles or yourself for Full Moon rituals. It can also be used when you feel like you need the moons energy.

Moon Water Tonic

Items needed

1 cup Purified Water

Clear Quartz

Clear Glass

Clear Plastic Wrap

Directions

Wait for a clear night, if possible, on or right in advance of the Full Moon. In a clear glass Place your crystal and add the purified water. At sundown, set the glass outdoors in a moonlit area and cover the glass with the clear plastic wrap. At dawn, remove the glass. The tonic water is now imbued with lunar potency.

You will drink the moon water tonic each morning to prepare yourself the pressure of your day.

NINE

Waning Moon Spells

A Spell to Bind Bullies

ITEMS NEEDED

3 Black Candles
Black Thread
Empty Glass Jar with Lid
Black Pen
Piece of Paper
Candle Snuffer

Directions

For reference, this spell will not injure your bully, it will simply cause them leave you alone. Perform this spell at midnight on a Saturday of a waning moon

Place the candles in a large triangle, large enough so that you can sit in the center.

Light your candles. Write the bully's name on your paper, followed by drawing an X over it.

Fold it three times away from you. Declare:

"I bind you (state their name)

So that you cannot harm me any longer,

Not only physically, but also emotionally.

Go away, leave me alone.

I bind you (state their name) I bind you."

Tie the thread around the folded paper, and drop it in the jar Snuff out the candles with candle snuffer or any non-flammable object that will close the flame. You never, want to blow out your candles after a spell; it tends to drives the magick from you). You can put the black candles you used in the jar if they are small enough and then Screw on the lid. The following day, bury the jar off your property, or you can conceal it in a closet somewhere it will not be discovered. If your candles are not small enough to fit in the jar, burn them afterward until there is nothing left of them.

Break a Bad Habit

Items needed

Black candle

Black Pen

23 Pieces of Paper

Directions

On the piece of paper, write down the habit that you wish to be rid of. Light the candle, and staring into the flame as you clear your head of all thinking. Grab hold of the paper and burn it with the candle, while reciting:

"With this purging flame, I expel you from my life

So mote it be."

After you have done this, you are ready to express a new goal. Taking the other piece of paper, you will write down. Be sure your new goal is positive, and written in the present tense. Such as, "I am happy every day. My body is healthy," etc. you are going to do this every morning for 21 days on a different piece of paper.

Candle Spell to Stop Annoyance

Items needed
Brown Image Candle or Plain Brown Candle
Honey
Pen
Parchment Paper
Your Athame, Small Knife, or Pin

Directions
Use a brown image candle, if you can otherwise a regular brown one will do fine, to signify the individual who is annoying you. Inscribe the person's name on the front as well as the back of your candle. On the piece of parchment paper, write:

"From now on, (state their name) will speak nothing but sweet words to me and about me.

By the strength of Aradia, so mote it be!"

Place a glob of honey in the center of the paper then roll it into a ball.

Warm up, your Athame, small knife, or pin and then if it is an image candle, make a cut in its mouth, or simply in the candle and fill your paper ball in it. Allow the candle burn a little every evening for an odd amount of nights up to a full nine nights. Toss the leftovers into moving water, but keep some of the candle droppings or ash from paper to scatter in the footpath of your tormentor.

Spell to Becoming Debt-Free

Items needed
Myrrh Oil
White Pillar Candle
Pen and Paper
Pin

Directions

During a new or waning moon, write a list of precisely what you owe, and whom you owe it to. After you have made this list on the paper, carve the same list into the candle with the pin. Inscribe the candle with all of your debts, and then add a drop or two of oil onto it. Light the candle and calm your thoughts as best you can. Look into the flame of the candle, visualizing your debts evaporating away. See yourself paying off your last debts, your accounts paid and being filled with feelings of independence and simplicity. Sit with this visualization for ten minutes. Let the candle burn for ten more minutes. Repeat this each night until the candle has burned down completely. You should soon see yourself out of debt, unexpected money or a way to save money that can help pay off your debt.

Conclusion

For centuries, dating back to ancient times, people have harnessed the moon's power and bathed in its silver light. In ancient times, the moon would be used to guide people in the planting of crops, the harvesting of crops, hunting, and even relationships.

Man has long since been fascinated with heavenly bodies, especially the moon, which patiently follows the earth in its journey around the sun, giving shadow and light when necessary. At the same time, it helps the tides brush along the shores. The moon can offer a person a lot of comforts, enhance a person" magick, and help them achieve a deeper spiritual understanding.

Once you know how to harness its powers, you will be able to reflect its light from within you. You will find peace, tranquility, and be able to enhance your magick by focusing on the moon's light. But as with anything, learning how to harness the moon's magick takes practice, patience, and perseverance. What you start, you must remember you need to always follow through by accepting the courage, power, and grace from the magick of the moon.

When drawing power from the moon or working magick

Conclusion

blessed by its power, always remember to be courteous to the Goddesses helping you guide the energies. Always give thanks to the moon as a heavenly body and as the Goddess who grants you a path to these powers.

Be generous to yourself and others, and have faith in yourself and your abilities as you grow with the moon from its lunar rebirth to full maturity.

May the moon's light always comfort, bless, and guide you.

References

Annulus (n.). (n.d.). Online Etymology Dictionary. https://www.etymonline.com/word/annulus

Burns, J. (2018, April 10). What Are the Eight Phases of the Moon in Order? Sciencing. https://sciencing.com/eight-phases-moon-order-6329177.html

Earth's Moon. (n.d.). NASA Science. https://solarsystem.-nasa.gov/moons/earths-moon/lunar-phases-and-eclipses/#:~:text=These%20eight%20phas-es%20are%2C%20in,third%20quarter%20and%20waning%20crescent.

Facts About the Moon. (2004, July 16). National Geographic. https://www.nationalgeographic.com/sci-ence/2004/07/moon-facts/#:~:text=The%20moon's%20-gravitational%20pull%20on,and%20the%20pull%20is%20weakest.

Hocken, V. (n.d.). When Is the Next Blue Moon? timeand-date.com. https://www.timeanddate.com/astrono-my/moon/blue-moon.html

Howell, E. (2019, January 22). What Is a Blood Moon? Space.com. https://www.space.com/39471-what-is-a-blood-moon.html

Howell, E. (2020, April 06). What Is a Supermoon? Space.com. https://www.space.com/38940-supermoon-facts.html

Our Ancient Obsession With Capturing the Moon. (2019, July 19). Science Friday. https://www.sciencefriday.com/segments/moon-art-history/

Rao, J. (2017, April 25). Total Solar Eclipses: How Often Do They Occur (and Why)? Space.com. https://www.space.com/25644-total-solar-eclipses-frequency-explained.html

What Is Moon Magic? (n.d.). Sage Goddess. https://www.sagegoddess.com/full-moon-magic/

About the Author

Monique Joiner Siedlak is a writer, witch, and warrior on a mission to awaken people to their greatest potential through the power of storytelling infused with mysticism, modern paganism, and new age spirituality. At the young age of 12, she began rigorously studying the fascinating philosophy of Wicca. By the time she was 20, she was self-initiated into the craft, and hasn't looked back ever since. To this day, she has authored over 40 books pertaining to the magick and mysteries of life.

To find out more about Monique Joiner Siedlak artistically, spiritually, and personally, feel free to visit her **official website**.

www.mojosiedlak.com

facebook.com/mojosiedlak

x.com/mojosiedlak

instagram.com/mojosiedlak

pinterest.com/mojosiedlak

bookbub.com/authors/monique-joiner-siedlak

More Books by Monique

African Spirituality Beliefs and Practices
Hoodoo
Seven African Powers: The Orishas
Cooking for the Orishas
Lucumi: The Ways of Santeria
Voodoo of Louisiana
Haitian Vodou
Orishas of Trinidad
Connecting with your Ancestors
Blood Magick
The Orishas
Vodun: West Africa's Spiritual Life
Marie Laveau: Life of a Voodoo Queen
Candomblé: Dancing for the God
Umbanda
Exploring the Rich and Diverse World

Divination Magic for Beginners
Divination with Runes
Divination with Diloggún
Divination with Osteomancy

Divination with the Tarot
Divination with Stones

The Beginner's Guide to Inner Growth
Astral Projection for Beginners
Meditation for Beginners
Reiki for Beginners

Mastering Your Inner Potential
Creative Visualization
Manifesting With the Law of Attraction

Holistic Healing and Energy
Healing Animals with Reiki
Crystal Healing
Communicating with Your Spirit Guides

Empathic Understanding and Enlightenment
Being an Empath Today

Life on Fire
Healing Your Inner Child
Change Your Life
Raising Your Vibe

The Indie Author's Guides
The Indie Author's Guide to Fast Drafting Your Novel

Get a Handle on Life
Get a Handle on Stress
Time Bound
Get a Handle on Anxiety
Get a Handle on Depression
Get a Handle on Procrastination

The Holistic Yoga and Wellness Series

Yoga for Beginners
Yoga for Stress
Yoga for Back Pain
Yoga for Weight Loss
Yoga for Flexibility
Yoga for Advanced Beginners
Yoga for Fitness
Yoga for Runners
Yoga for Energy
Yoga for Your Sex Life
Yoga to Beat Depression and Anxiety
Yoga for Menstruation
Yoga to Detox Your Body
Yoga to Tone Your Body

The DIY Body Care Series

Creating Your Own Body Butter
Creating Your Own Body Scrub
Creating Your Own Body Spray

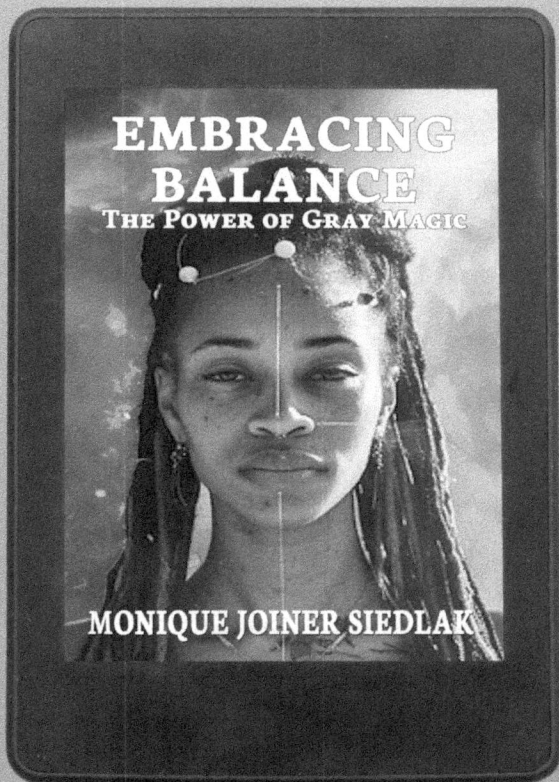

SUPPORT ME BY LEAVING A REVIEW!

goodreads

amazon

BookBub

Download on
Apple Books

GET IT ON
Google Play

nook
by Barnes & Noble

Rakuten
kobo